Reflected Fractures

Poems

By Ren Kato

ISBN: 978-0-6452199-0-6

Cover photo and design: Briea Hope

CONTENTS

Watercolours

The same tortured faces
frequent this establishment
Watercolours of the apocalypse
adorn the faded wall
Lonely eyes scream
cacophonous music
She laments another lost love
There's nothing but heartache in this town

Modern Letters

Driving down these electronic superhighways
I'll meet you where you are
We don't have to wait for days
I'll always write these modern letters to you

Can you feel the city's rapid pulse now?
Laser beams of nightclub debauchery
Nam June Paik predicted the future somehow
Connected to the machine, message seen

You're in a different galaxy
but I'm glad we can still talk
Love in the modern age
is like dancing with a broken rib cage

half the time

Field of lights
What does the futurist fear?
Taking photos with your phone,
you wait for your clone

What does the future hold for this
digital age dream?

Connect the Dots

Attempting to connect the dots
but it all becomes
more obfuscated
The haze burns your skin
Doctor said
that the remedy is gin?

Darkness enveloping plastic plants
and carcasses
Reflections of apparitions
in the window
Capturing the mood
with your camera
Unburdened by time
I traverse the spiral staircase
of your face

// my psychosis worsens
in this room of darkness //

Won't you turn on the light,
my love?

Endless

An endless stream
of conversations
on that handheld device
yet these scars
of lonesomeness
still cause her grief

Another night
with the heater on
but it's still
far too cold

Summoning
the faint memory
of that one time
she was in love

Human

Your friends hide in your phone
Their words have lost all meaning

You wonder
what you would do
if there was nothing left to stream
Cybernetic dream
More android than human

'Don't separate me from my
devices, take my heart instead.'

Humdrum

Another humdrum night.

binge-watching shows,

eating leftovers,

checking my phone, and drinking beer

The screen paralyses my eyes.

Digital Age Dream

This digital age
It's never been easier
to stay connected
yet I still feel
isolated
The text messages I read
written by those friends I rarely see
I absorb the view of the city
from the driver's seat of
my dilapidated car
An ad for the latest technologies
Better get the next iPhone,
computer and
virtual reality headset
The purpose of life is to
escape reality. Perhaps?
Perhaps not.
Drinking alone in empty bars
The android bartender
looks at me
like I don't belong
Was there an exodus
of the human race
I did not hear about?
No, I know everyone's at home,
exploring the virtual world
Reality became too real for them

Consume

Basically everything is online these days
literature, love, entertainment,
your hourly news fix,
and more.

Blink and you'll get punched
collect these metaphorical stars from the cosmos

Pitch-Black

You didn't find your soul
during that last bender
but such disappointment
will not stop you
from trying again tonight

Sending drunken texts
to mend the torment of heartache

It is a story that
goes nowhere

A bare-knuckle fight
makes you feel alive

Ending the night
in a dirty dive bar
waiting for the sun
to gift you revelations
alcohol won't provide

Murder at a Dinner Party

There was a murder at a dinner party
but nobody noticed it
they were all on their phones
The body never got cleaned up

Let's take a breather
and watch the meteor shower
     What an opulent night
     Wouldn't you agree?

Your eyes navigate the screen
     as I talk

Let's go for a drive
down these forgotten highways
and pretend nothing's changed after all these years

You just uploaded your hundredth self-portrait
     to your online gallery
Surely your followers know
what you look like by now
     That new angle doesn't change much
I just know you can't get enough
of people commenting
     on how good you look
  Baby, narcissism doesn't suit you

Crush your phone with a brick

And let's go for a drive
down these forgotten highways
and pretend nothing has changed
after all these years

Noxious Haze

Lacerated days
(writing a book of essays)
On the crowded train
with cognitive malaise
quickly traversing through
society's noxious haze

My eyes roam
(beyond the lens of my illusory home)
they catch the deep
gaze of the maiden sitting alone
tell me all about your hedonist phase
then save my number to your phone

Beatnik chic

She dances with

poetic subtlety

in the humid club

as it starts to collapse

The comfort of her tongue

She knows

how to get things done

She's interstellar

beatnik chic,

looks like she hasn't slept

all week

Philosophical organism

Show me your architecture
I want to understand you
completely
philosophical organism
Those curtains fall
but the play continues
It is about drifters
who have no home,
no nation to call their own

Are you just like them?
    A citizen of nowhere?

Scarred Tongue

I wrote a few poems
about the apocalypse
but all I really wanted
was to kiss her lips
which I did
in the booth of some polluted dive bar

It took some time
but I solved the
riddle.

The moon begins to disintegrate
Conversations about
Planet Earth and fate

She was somehow
impressed by my words
Even though I thought
they were absurd

What drew her to this soul
that was stuck in a grey landscape,
slowly bleeding from a wound of existential dread?

Soundscapes

Music plays in the apartment
(the ambient crooning of Dirty Beaches)
This kind of music
is perfect for this time of night
Where are we exactly? I'm not sure.
This city reminds me of home
Wine and cigarettes satisfy
our late night cravings
I look out from the balcony
watching a brawl break out
10/10 entertainment
Traffic congestion and
pedestrians consuming
a variety of street food
after a session of heavy drinking
amongst other debaucherous rituals

Wait

I see your face in every painting
and hear your heartbeat from oceans away
I wish I could board a flight to see you
but it's a pipe dream right now
We just have to wait

Phantasms

Drinking wine with the
phantasms of my mind
I'll sleep at sunrise

Engrave

I engrave my name into your skull
You engrave your name into mine
A trip to the future on your soft tongue
Your eyes change colour everyday
You learn a new language every year

You're from a town I've never heard of
where people crave to see stars on a black canvas
The closest supermarket
feels like it's in another continent
Everything about your home bores you now
It might as well be the loneliest place on earth
Stuck in this empty scene,
yearning to swim in the city illuminations of Osaka

PYRAMID

An ancient Egyptian pyramid appears on the serene beach.

I see it en route to nowhere. Of course I take some pictures for social media. 2am. Is there anyone I can call? Is there? The world is so much more beautiful after dark. Ocean waves – like an orchestra to my ears. Picasso sold some paintings at the markets earlier today. Everything looks like a cubist painting to him. Sometimes I get the urge to live out at sea. There aren't too many reasons for me to be here. What happened to those friends I never see? We made plans that were never followed through. I've heard stories about overdose and death. Let's fade away into that perfect utopia and meditate with drunken angels on the tranquil beach.

Lounge Room Surrealism

Watch out, there are holes in the ground and lions in the
lounge room

Blood taints your glass of water, teeth swimming in your
tomato soup

Cataclysm of those nocturnal eyes, might be going blind

You won't be online tonight

Nobody Should Drink Champagne Alone

Cigarette smoke
taking the form of
the one you desire
the most
In your high-rise apartment
$1000 rent per week
The moon writes a letter
to the sun
You drink champagne
alone
New text message
Can't remember
your phone's passcode

Mistress of Despair

Love is the mistress of despair
                     It takes a lot to care
                              Love is the mistress of despair
Tell me, what am I going to find there
              on the moon of her cosmic eyes?
                              I killed my fears with red wine
How will it all end?
          For now, shall we go see the places from
                         your favourite documentaries?

Quiet City

A public execution
outside city hall
Cruel consciousness
The magic trick of reality
Skeleton trees swaying in the wind
of a hot night
what a gruesome summer
Dracula in his new Versace suit
is on the hunt for blood
You have seen your future play out on screen
Starry-eyed socialites
visiting from outer space
in the queue outside the venue
They could've gone anywhere in the universe
and yet they chose this city
Decomposed rats in the gutter, metres away
Did you see Jack the Ripper
walking the streets in sneakers
slitting throats of harlots?
Blood stains the path to enlightenment
Another awful band on stage
The humdrum noise of metropolitan streets
is preferable to this
The goddess of love drinks alone
in the smoking area outside,
reading Sylvia Plath's
Mad Girl's Love Song
on her phone

A smile that only shows despair
These poets observe the streets
An ad for the latest high-rise apartment
catches your eye
sadly the price is too high
Paranoid about the future
You were promised the world
a long time ago
you thought you'd be living in a
mansion with a Basquiat painting
on the wall
but you're struggling just to pay rent
I'm sure you'll solve your
paralysing problems
Mia the murderer buries bodies
in the garden of the heartbreak hotel
I see my name on one of the tombstones
I grab my coat and duffle bag
and speed down the highway
in sixth gear
with the past decaying away
not to be remembered
I've crafted a new mask to wear
I'm an illusion I've created for myself

REVERB

Putrid sky spilling oil, angels assassinating everyone they
see, barbarians running amok, this modern city
turning into ancient ruins

Finding peace of mind in Buddhist philosophy
Doing all I can to survive
in a world that continues to decay

Currently

Kicking skulls along the road,
beyond the buskers and taxi rank.
This hazy half-moon delights you
Look, another venue out of business
What will open up next?
These streets are always changing
Is it a slow death of soundless horror?

I dreamt of
the different ways I could die
You fantasised about
the various ways you could get high
Those angels who got kicked out of heaven
are brawling outside the strip club
on Queen Street

A rendezvous with our friends
in the same bar as always
Let's just get out of here
and go to Vietnam
It is one of the countries
I call home
A life of routine is a pain
The music in here is bad for the soul
They used to play good shit
What happened to this place?

The completion of the ritual

To be out of the house and
around others can be
exhausting

Need some time to heal
The melting of the silver spoon
I escape into my mind's lagoon
until I'm rudely interrupted by
reality, once again

Sinister Angel

corpses under the sun
trembling roses
the day started out fun
now animals drink
from a river of blood
take my breath away,
sinister angel

Grotesque Places

This city's fragrance
smells cheap these days
café coffee doesn't taste
the same
Too many carcasses
on the street
Where are the vultures
to clean everything up?
The bars we frequented
have closed down
only the grotesque
establishments have
managed to survive
Your favourite singer
doesn't perform with
the same feeling
anymore

Living Room

I use his skull as a decoration in my living room. Paintings I stole hang on the walls throughout my house. I stare at the Starry Night with a glass of wine before I cascade into a half-baked slumber. Next time you're here, I'll take you on a walk through Nam June's TV Garden. Block those fools you see on your feed. Drink wine during summer nights, and talk about the past. There is no story here, just random occurrences. Stay informed. Change what you can. Analyse architecture. Read poetry. Spy on the spies. Have you noticed the cattle have morphed into wolves?

Mirror

A million birds flying through
the light of a sorrowful moon
Nobody notices the dying flowers
on the coffee table
Skeletons using enemy blood
to draw pictures depicting war
Blood drips from the universe's
eyeball
I write poetry to keep my soul alive

Ocean

Her mind swims
in an ocean of
torturous loneliness

She senses her soul dying
more and more
with every drink

Staring at art
from the Edo Period,
waiting for Hokusai's Wave
to wash the sins
of humanity away

Concrete

you sleep on cold concrete

       a crow attacks   and   steals an eye

your   lover   approaches

              takes   your   heart

then

      donates it to the museum of loneliness

it's just one of those days

EDO

Laying on the concrete
with a broken neck
I wish I could help
that person getting
chased by a lion

This city is where
humanity's final novel
was written
The bohemians have
vanished
reincarnated into corporate hounds

I don't want to be trapped
I'd rather be a vagabond
even if it means being poor

As soon as I recover,
I plan to leave this civilisation
and travel back in time
to Edo period Japan
where I will be a travelling poet
Maybe I'll meet Yosa Buson
and my ancestors

Blade

Blood on the blade
She's dangerous
Someday she'll be famous

When she dies
The empire she created will mourn
Buried in the town where her mother was born

Dreams echoing into the next life

Lunar Surface

Memories of the apocalypse disappear
every time I look
into her eyes

Our home planet committed suicide
    due to society's treatment

'Where do you want to go?'
I asked her. 'We could go to the moon, Mars
or to some other galaxy.'

My baby lives dangerously
She handcuffed her wrist
to a briefcase full of drugs
A never-ending supply
Downtime in the sauna
She loves to share but only with me
Eager to live but not afraid to die
Wants to enjoy her time
Her stint in rehab was spent
getting high
The kind of girl who'll die young
yet be remembered forever

She and I went to sleep
Woke up on the lunar surface
I have no idea what we inhaled
into our lungs

She could not get
any Internet connection
which inspired various complaints
'Why couldn't you just enjoy the view
from the moon?'
At least we escaped city ghosts and politics

Metropolitan

She paints
metropolitan nights
on a canvas
as it rains outside
I've forgotten what the city
looks like
We listen to music
of an existential nature
and read the poetry of
Li Bai
in a cabin away from
civilisation

Moonstruck

You gave me a painting
by Picasso
I would have preferred
one of yours

I'm moonstruck
by you
I wish I had
stars to gift you

I'm a lonely astronaut
lost in your orbit

Powerful empires
eventually fall
but the empire of
our love is forevermore

Gambling Den

Restless tremor of fate
decided at the gambling den

Drinking gin
lost in a ruminative state

Do you have an appointment
at the cemetery gates?

I wait for those cards to be dealt

Untitled

Washing hands with oil paint

Rent's late, tempting fate

You haven't touched drugs since 2008

yet dealers still wait by the gate

Stalking you as if you're prey

Final words from your lover

One tragedy after another, it is

all about what you can endure

I've only ever seen your face in pictures

and reflections

I bet I would find you in the

philosophy section

of some vintage book store

in a city that always rains

Books containing

the meaning of life

sold for ten bucks each

Wisdom has never been so cheap

night poem

She spent the night
looking for
spirits in the graveyard
ended up burying
her beating heart
she now has a scythe
and a loaded gun

Before She Goes

Meditating as the tsunami hits
It's the end of an era
The cops still haven't found the killer
All the signs say to go in all directions
They dig deep to find oil
I endeavour to find the ghost
of ancient ruins
while she savours
every breath

I recite the poem I wrote for her
then play our favourite song
This is the last time
she gets to listen to music
I kiss my love on her deathbed
The end is here

Music Perfect for a Funeral

Deathbed conversations
I hear rogue angels singing
Your summertime playlist
- music perfect for a funeral
It's difficult to breathe outside
This dilapidated house is where we hide

Ancient phantasms
have stopped haunting me
Some memories are better forgotten
With you here, I've neglected my devices
You've robbed me of an existential crisis

Psychopathic Princess

Psychopathic princess, give me your tongue
Don't provoke me, just show me I'm the only one
My melancholic heart yearns,
the fields burn
My town is
nothing but ash now
It's time to rebuild

ABOUT THE AUTHOR

Ren Kato was born in Japan, and raised in Australia.

He is of Vietnamese and Japanese descent.

Reflected Fractures is his first poetry collection.

www.ingramcontent.com/pod-product-compliance
Lightning Source LLC
Chambersburg PA
CBHW060540030426
42337CB00021B/4363